Norse Mythology

Tales of Norse Gods, Heroes, Beliefs, Rituals & the Viking Legacy.

Dale Hansen

Table of Contents

Introduction

On June 8th of the year 793 A.D., the inhabitants of the small island named Lindisfarne became the first Christians in the British Isles to encounter and record an attack by those whom we now know as the Vikings. No one had suspected that an attack from the sea by mainlanders was possible. As it was, St. Aidan's little church on Lindisfarne was destroyed and many islanders were killed or captured, marking the beginning of the "Viking Age."

From where did the Vikings come? Who were they and what forces shaped their lives? These questions seemed less relevant then than they are to our interest now. Indeed, perhaps these questions are of even greater interest now that many parts of English-speaking worlds and cultures at large have been influenced and shaped by the Vikings. Today, we add questions about Viking culture and beliefs that the peoples of the Medieval Ages did not have the freedom to investigate.

In this book, we will learn about new discoveries of historians and archaeologists about Viking culture to which the people of the Viking Age were not privy. The flattened picture that many have depicted concerning Viking beliefs and practices will illustrate to us a three-dimensional landscape full of subtlety and depth. We will overturn modern myths of Vikings as uncultured barbarians with horned helmets spending all their days raping, pillaging, and plundering to see the deep culture and complex belief system beneath. We will begin to see parallels to modern culture and, indeed, we will find Viking influence on many aspects of our own, modern practices, beliefs, language and pastimes.

Chapter One: Viking Origins

The Viking Age officially began on record in 793 A.D. with the downfall of the Christian island of Lindisfarne to Viking invaders. However, this was not the genesis of Viking culture. The beginnings of human culture in southern Scandinavia can be traced back to the end of the last Ice Age, with agriculture developed around 4000 B.C., the Bronze Age starting around 2000 B.C., and the Iron Age emerging around 500 B.C., much in parallel with the main continent of Europe.

Previous Cultures

The Maglemosian people of 9000 to 6000 B.C. seem to have been the earliest direct human ancestors of the Vikings. They emerged in the Scandinavian north after the last Ice Age. Out of the Maglemose came the Kongemosen culture of great hunters in Sweden and Denmark and the Nostvet culture in Norway. They predate the Vikings by thousands of years, and likely were ancestors to the cultures of the more modern Norse, Swedes, and Danes.

The Kongemose and Nostvet cultures became the Ertebolle culture. The Ertebolle people were exceptional hunter-gatherers, fishers, and pottery-makers. There exists evidence of conflict in the Ertebolle culture, as some skeletons in Sweden and Zealand contain arrowheads inside their remains. There is also evidence of cannibalism. It is likely that the Ertebolle culture was more sedentary than nomadic, as shown by the cemeteries that archaeologists have found from the Mesolithic Period.

The Ertebolle grew in parallel with and was replaced by the Swifterbant culture, which lasted a bit longer until 3400 B.C., and whose people learned a bit of animal husbandry and agriculture. The Swifterbant people raised both cows and pigs as well as emmer wheat and barley.

Proto-Viking Culture

As the Bronze Age emerged, we have more evidence of Scandinavian culture but still very little from which to draw conclusions. Archaeologists have studied various carvings from the period and have found that, unsurprisingly, the people of early Scandinavia were great seafarers. In addition, carved images from the period show that the Scandinavian cultures were full of fighting and raiding, another conclusion that might not surprise us.

Bogs have preserved and given us clues as to the culture as early as 350 B.C., but very little can be established for certain. The Hjortspring Boat, for example, is the earliest evidence of a plank vessel in Europe and shows us that Viking ancestors were advanced boat-builders.

During Europe's Migration Period in the first millennium A.D., the Vikings formed their culture and, toward the end of the Migration Period, saw the start of the Viking Age. At the beginning of this period, Scandinavians generally lived in small, rural settlements and fished, farmed, and fought one another from these locations. With time, these settlements were organized into chiefdoms with centers of power in places such as Eketorp on the Swedish island of Oland and Gamla Uppsala ("Old" Uppsala) in Uppland, Sweden. Large burial mounds are still evident in Gamla Uppsala and are a testament the transition from small tribes to regional territories ruled by kings.

The last part of the Scandinavian Iron Age is called the Vendel Period, and it lasted from 600 to 800 A.D. During this period, the people buried their kings in their ships along with many fine objects, a tradition that lasted into the Viking Age.

Sources for Learning about Viking History and Culture

Some of what we learn about the Vikings is from outside sources, that is, from the cultures that interacted with the Vikings that were their Scandinavian neighbors. For example, Saxo Grammaticus wrote *Gesta Danorum*, "The Story of the Danes," in which he described the three Scandinavian regions, Norway, Denmark, and Sweden, where the Vikings lived. While Saxo was himself a Dane, born in Zealand, he was of the Roman Catholic faith, and thus an outsider to Viking culture.

Adam of Bremen is another source, especially for learning about the religious practices of the Viking culture. It is said he never attended a religious ceremony in Gamla Uppsala, but he is supposed to have interviewed many faithful witnesses and thus gives us what he claims is an accurate portrayal of Viking religious traditions.

The "inside sources" that we can access are mostly oral traditions. The Scandinavians spoke Old Norse and used a runic alphabet system with 16 characters, but most runic script was relegated to denoting ownership, such as "Melbrigda owns this brooch," or to marking tombstones. Runic writing was developed for carving into wood or bone but eventually came to be used on metal and stone as well. However, because it was a tedious process, runes were not used for recording any more than short events in history.

Rather than learning the culture and history of the Vikings from runes, we learn it from oral poems, which were eventually written down as sagas in the 13th century. There were two types of poetry that the Scandinavians used to record information and history: The *Poetic Edda* was one form of poetry. It is a collection of 39 Old Norse poems that were gathered and compiled in 13th century Iceland. There was also the *Prose Edda*, which was gathered and written down by Snorri Sturluson, a 13th century Icelandic author.

The other form of poetry was "skaldic poetry," for which Snorri Sturluson was most famous. A "skald" was a poet from Iceland who used verses to recount current or historical events along with the people involved. Sturluson himself wrote *Heimskringla*, of which the famous *Ynglinga Saga* was a part. The Ynglinga were an important family from the famed Gamla Uppsala, and it seems that Sturluson created a few kings to fill in the gaps between three real kings' reigns to make the story more interesting.

No matter what the sources of our information, we must submit to the fact that the lives of the Vikings were just as human and therefore just as complex as any other ancient civilizations, as well as comparable to the humanity and complexity of our lives today. The Vikings had little technology, certainly very little in comparison to our level of advancement in present time, but their complicated religious system more than balances in subtlety and depth of influence. The Vikings' social and spiritual pressures might seem foreign to us, but I hope we will learn to see a reflection of our own hopes and desires in them.

Chapter Two: Famed Battles, Wars, and Sieges

The Vikings grew infamous among the rest of the Europeans for their ferocity and ruthlessness in battle and for their customs of raping and pillaging in seaside villages. Though this is a flattened conception of the Vikings, the full picture is not less than these things, but rather adds certain dimensions to these truths. Vikings indeed were fearsome warriors, and a person current to their time would not want to underestimate their prowess in battle.

The Vikings' strength in war as well as their element of surprise lent them great success in conquest. In the East on mainland Europe, in Britain, in Ireland, and in North America, the Vikings found success overcoming and having dominion over the native peoples for various amounts of time.

Mainland Europe – In the East

The Scandinavians traded in the Baltic Sea region since the 600's A.D., but they did not attack until the mid-9th century. Their attack was unexpected because of their peaceful relations with the Baltic people previously. They remained mostly traders and settlers in the East afterward, though they established themselves as preeminent over the native peoples rather quickly.

As they settled into the Slavic culture surrounding them, they began to assimilate, leading to the Vikings no longer being considered Vikings. The ones that remained in Scandinavia lent their services as mercenaries to the Slavs in Novgorod and Kiev, however, still were known as fearsome warriors.

Novgorod – 852 A.D.

The first recorded attack by the Scandinavian Vikings in the East took place in 852, much later than the attack on Lindisfarne. In this attack, Swedish Vikings overtook the city of Novgorod and demanded a large tax from the citizens.

Within six years, by 858 A.D., the Vikings became the rulers over the *Rus*, the native Slavic peoples, and settled themselves in Kiev. They became known to the *Rus* as well as to the Byzantines and to the Arabs as *Varangians*.

Attacks on Constantinople – 860 A.D. and later

In 860 A.D., the Vikings launched an attack on the city they called *Miklagard*, otherwise known as Constantinople. The Viking attackers sailed down the Dnieper River and across the Black Sea to reach the famed city, but they were unsuccessful in their assault of the city. By the time they reattempted their efforts in the early and mid-900's, the Vikings were assimilated into the Slavic *Rus* population, so it was not considered an attack by Vikings.

Vikings in England

The attack on Lindisfarne was the first assault by Vikings in England that has been discovered in records from the time. For about 40 years after the attack on Lindisfarne, there was a period of calm, which was in turn shattered by at attack on Sheppey by the Vikings. Nearly every year that followed the English recorded attacks by the Scandinavians, and by 855 A.D., the Vikings began to stay the winters on English soil.

The Avenging of Ragnar Lodbrok and What Ensued – Ninth Century A.D.

Ragnar "Hairy Breeches" Lodbrok was considered by the Vikings the epitome of a Viking king. Thus, when he was killed in the 850's A.D., his sons and their men sought vengeance for his death, blaming his execution on King Aella of Northumbria in England instead of on the Norse king in Ireland who was the more likely suspect.

Ragnar Lodbrok's sons, including Ivar the Boneless, Halfdan, and Ubbi, also known as Hubba, launched an attack on York in 867 A.D and executed King Aella the next year. In 869, Ivar had King Edmund in East Anglia executed and subsequently disappeared, probably to Dublin, Ireland. Halfdan took charge of the Viking army, consisting of a king, five jarls and their men, and all by Halfdan were killed in the Battle of Ashdown in 871.

Despite the devastating loss at Ashdown, Halfdan went on to defeat the English summarily in the next many battles. Eventually, after setting up some puppet kings in England, Halfdan sailed to Ireland where he was killed in the Battle of Strangford Lough in 877 A.D.

Guthrum and the Peace of 886

In his stead, a Viking named Guthrum took over the Danish forces in England. He was accompanied by two kings, Oskytel and Anwend. In 878, Guthrum came extremely close to overtaking the final independent Saxon kingdom, under King Alfred.

Instead, however, Alfred made a comeback with his army and eventually forced Guthrum to accept the Peace of 886 after the Battle of Edington. In this treaty, the two leaders established an area that would eventually be known as "Danelaw," the area of England under Viking occupation.

Brunanburh, 937 A.D. – Gift to Mercenary Economy

In 937 A.D., a marked change in the Vikings' battle economy began to be apparent. The gift economy by which the Vikings operated, such that loyalties were established by extravagant gifts, began to turn into a mercenary economy.

King Athelstan hired Egil Skallagrimson and his brother, Thorolf, to help fight in the battle against the northern kings. Athelstan manipulated the battle in such a way that Thorolf and his men were brutally slaughtered, and Egil Skallagrimson was only appeased when Athelstan gave him an expensive gold arm band.

Maldon, 991 A.D.

The Vikings had been in continual defeat for about a century by the time of Battle of Maldon. Instead of bringing a small raiding force, like they had been doing, the Viking brought 93 ships of men, probably several thousand warriors in total, along for the attack.

Byrhtnoth led the troops of Essex against the invading forces, and, being overambitious, led many to their deaths, including himself. He left his horse in the charge of a man named Godric, who promptly jumped astride the horse and fled. The rest of the troops of Essex mistook Godric for Byrhtnoth and fled as well, leaving Byrhtnoth to be killed by a javelin.

As a result of the loss to the Vikings, the King Ethelred of Essex was required to pay increasing Danegeld sums, which funded national efforts by the Danes to expand their influence in the early 11th century.

Fulford, 1066 A.D.

Harald Sigurdsson, nicknamed *Hardradi,* or "the Ruthless," joined forces with the Earl Tostig, who had decided to return from exile and march on the English throne. There were about 300 Viking ships under Harald's command, according to the *Anglo-Saxon Chronicle,* amassing around 10,000 men. Earl Tostig added his own 12 ships and many men, and together they marched on Fulford, which they promptly defeated. York then opened negotiations with Harald without any show of resistance.

Stamford Bridge, 1066 A.D.

To accept the hostages whom Harold Godwinsson agreed to hand over, the Vikings under Harald Sigurdsson came ashore without armor at Stamford Bridge. They were very unpleasantly surprised when King Harold Godwinsson came with an army instead of with the hostages. The Vikings went into a war frenzy but Harald fell and soon the entire Viking force was defeated.

Harald Sigurdsson is called the "last Viking" because this was the end of the Viking Age. Nearly 300 years of Viking dominance came to an end with a terrible battle, as the Vikings would likely have it no other way. An entry into Valhalla.

Vikings in Ireland

The Vikings first arrived in Ireland in 795 A.D., when they plundered the island called Reachrann, ransacking two monasteries that stood there. After 830 A.D., the Vikings intensified their efforts to take control of Ireland, and they started to truly colonize around 840. After that point, Dublin was the center of Viking power in Ireland with its own self-appointed kings. The Vikings were then drawn into Irish politics and pitted themselves for and against various petty Irish kings.

Clontarf, 1014 A.D.

Brian Boru was a chieftain who could claim that he was the king of Ireland for a period of history. Many Irish resented this fact, and rose against him. One of those who felt heavily offended by him was a man named Maelmordha of Leinster. He broke away for the winter and during that time the Battle of Clontarf occurred in which the Leinster leader, Maelmordha allied with the Vikings against Murchad's men and were defeated with heavy losses.

Many say this was the end of Viking power in Ireland, but it seems that it was not so decisive as that. The Scandinavian desire for conquest in Ireland did not cease with this battle, though it was many years before the Vikings came back to do battle in Ireland.

Vikings in North America

Historians agree that the Vikings reached Iceland in the Medieval Period of Europe. They might have even found Greenland at that point.

In 986 A.D., Bjarni Herjolfsson and his voyaging men were blown off course and sighted North America. Leif Eriksson came after in 1000 A.D. to a land they called *Helluland*, or "Flat Stone Land." This is now known as Baffin Island. The Viking seamen then discovered what we call Labrador, which they called *Markland*, or "Forest Land."

The Vikings' first settlement was called Leifsbudir, and upon further exploration, they discovered *Vinland*, the land of vines and grapes.

There were a few more trips to Vinland, including by Thorvald, Leif's brother. Their expedition was the first to encounter native people, whom they promptly killed. They called the aborigines *Skraelings*, or "screechers" or "wretches."

Another expedition settled in Vinland. The Vikings began to trade with the native people, until somehow relations turned sour and there was more fighting between the Viking and the Native Americans.

Inner-Viking Battles - Hafrsfjord, 872 A.D.

Harald Harfagri, the son of Halfdan the Black, overtook many parts of Norway by isolating and killing or subduing one king at a time. The Battle at Hafrsfjord occurred between the forces of Harald Harfagri and the loose alliance between Kjotvi the Wealthy and Thorir Longchin. It was a battle fought at sea, but it was different from many sea battles in that it was fought not by missile but by boarding each other's ships. Harald was known in this battle for having 12 berserkers, military men with presumed divine power to ignore attacks and to fight with raging ferocity. Having 12 of these men when one or two would have been considered formidable was what won Harald the battle.

What drove these battles, though? What belief systems and what understanding of the world was behind these ominous adventurers? This is what we will begin to explore next.

Chapter Three: Conception of the World – Yggdrasil, Creation, and the Afterlife

The informed, modern day person's understanding of the Vikings' conception of the world is summed up in the Old Norse word, "Yggdrasil." Yggdrasil is the tree that the Vikings believed holds the universe together. However, this is just one of numerous, separate but overlapping models that archaeologists have found in the Scandinavian world of their picture of the Earth and its surroundings.

Yggdrasil Conception

In the Yggdrasil model of the universe, Yggdrasil is a cosmic ash tree with three roots, which are representative of Hel (the land of the dead), Midgard (the world as we know it), and Utgard (the land of the giants and other troublesome creatures). There are then two bridges from the roots to the branches, which are Bif-rost, the trembling or swaying path, and As-bru, the bridge of the Ases. The branches represent Asgard, the land of the gods. A dragon is supposed to be eating at the roots of the tree, Yggdrasil, which accounts for the coming of the End Times, called Ragnarok, or the "fate of the gods."

Side-by-Side Conception

This conception, however, leaves out a few crucial elements of the Vikings' understanding of the world: Fenrir the cosmic wolf and the Midgard Serpent. In another model of the universe, Midgard is in the west and is separated by Eli-vagar (the "storm sea" river or river system) and Jarn-vidr (the "iron forest") from Utgard. This too is insufficient, because it also leaves out Fenrir and the Midgard Serpent.

Concentric Circles Conception

The another, varied conception that archaeologists have discovered among the Vikings is that of concentric circles of worlds. In the center, there is Midgard, the land of human beings and other creatures we are accustomed to encountering. Outside that is the primordial ocean, and within the ocean is the Midgard Serpent. Outside of the primordial ocean is Utgard, the land of giants. Within Midgard is a separate circle representing Asgard, and somewhere between Asgard and Midgard is chained Fenrir the wolf.

Nine Worlds Conception

In a variation on the concentric circles picture of the world, the Vikings believed that at the center of the universe was a tree, Yggdrasill, and that outside of the tree of Yggdrasill were concentric circles of worlds, of which Asgard and Midgard were two worlds. Jottunheim was another one of the nine total worlds and was the place where giants resided. Beneath the tree of Yggdrasill were still the three roots, of which Hel was still one. This nine world model seems the most complete of all the models.

However, likely, none of these conceptions alone clearly represents the Vikings' understanding of the earth and cosmos, but taking on the conceptions together, we gain some insight into their view of the world around them.

The next question is, how did the world come to be in the first place?

Creation

The Vikings believed that in the beginning, there existed something called the *ginnunga-gap*, or the "yawning void," a nothingness out of which something came to be. The giants are the oldest beings in existence, according to Norse mythology, and it was through the slaying of a giant named Ymir that the world was created.

Ymir's body was used to form the earth, the ocean came from Ymir's blood, mountains were made of bones, trees of the giant's hair, and the vaulted heavens came from the inside of Ymir's skull. The gods then used *Askr*, an ash tree and *Embla*, presumably a vine, and combined the two plants to create human beings.

Hans-Peter Hasenfratz points out in his book, *Barbarian Rituals*, that the Vikings' understanding of the creation of the world is similar to Indian and Iranian or Persian conceptions, and he also notes that the creation of human beings from a pair of plants comes through in Iranian mythology as well. As isolated as Viking culture was in its genesis and development, it influenced other peoples and was subject to influence by the surrounding cultures as well.

The Individual Afterlife – Valhalla, Folkvangr, and Hel

The afterlife of the dead who were slain in battle was split between Valhalla and Folkvangr. Half of the dead were led by the female Valkyries to Odin's hall called *Valhalla*, and half were consigned to spend their days on the field of *Folkvangr*, associated with Freyja.

Valhalla contained the masses of dead who died in combat and whom were known as *Einherjar*. Those entering the hall saw *Glasir*, the golden tree, upon entering, and, looking up, saw golden shields thatching the roof. A goat named *Heidrun* and a stag named *Eikpyrnir* lived around Valhalla and ate from the tree named *Laeradr*. In modern times, Valhalla has been reimagined as a pantheon like the dwelling of the Greek deities, but this is far from how the Vikings saw Valhalla.

The other half of the dead who died in battle were sent to Freyja's field called Folkvangr. The term means something like "people-field" or "army-field" and was thought to be no less prestigious than Valhalla. Freyja had built a hall named Sessrumnir for the dead that entered her realm. This was in parallel with Valhalla and was considered just as welcoming a death as entering Valhalla.

Hel was the last of the final destinations of people who had passed on, according to Viking beliefs. Hel was one belief that might have been influenced by Christian social and religious pressures. While Valhalla and Folkvangr were clearly of Norse origin and description, Snorri Sturluson's accounts of Hel seemed tinged by Christian influence according to many scholars. It is Snorri's assertion that those who die of illness or old age are directed to Hel, inspiring death in battle to traverse instead to Valhalla. However while the netherworld isn't explained often in different sources, its generally cast in a neutral or even positive belief.

Chapter Four: Viking Deities – The Ases

There are two types of deities in the Norse cosmology and mythology. The two classes of gods and goddesses are called the Ases, referring to the deities of Asgard, and the Wanes. As mentioned earlier in this book, neither set of deities were the original inhabitants of Yggdrasill or of this cosmos, according to Viking mythology, but rather the giants were the first living beings to take form in the world.

Relationship Between the Ases and the Wanes

After coming into being, the Ases arose and killed a giant named Ymir to create Midgard and the known world. The As deities learned harmful magic from one of the Wane goddesses, whom they proceeded to kill. This began a war between the Ases and the Wanes, the first war on Earth.

The Ases decided to build an unassailable fortress, or rather, decided to contract a giant to do this work for them within a year in return for a strong stallion. Loki the Trickster added that the Ases would provide the sun, the moon, and the Wane goddess, Freyja, one of Odin's lovers, as compensation as well.

When it became clear that the giant would finish in time, Loki turned into a giant, tempting mare to lead away the giant's stallion, and the giant turned on the Ases. Thor killed the giant, and in the aftermath, Heimdall the Guardian gave up his ear or sense of hearing to appease the Wanes. This entire conflict sealed the fate of the gods, called Ragnarok, in which they are destined to a fight that will end the world as we know it.

The moral of the story seems to be that the gods and goddesses of the Vikings were morally fallible, prone to gullibility in trusting Loki, to breaking oaths such as with the giant, and to warring amongst themselves. These stories would indicate that the Vikings believed that evil entered the world through the weakness of the gods themselves, for though they are powerful beings, they are prone to temptation just as humans are.

Even though each god wass considered morally fallible, the Vikings worshipped each of them in a unique way. Some of the more common and well-known, as well as more-worshipped of As deities include: Odin, Tyr, Thor, Loki, and Frigg. Let us investigate further into these gods' and goddesses' personalities and review some tales about them to gain insight into Viking culture and values.

Odin – The Chief God

Odin was the highest deity in the pantheon of the Vikings. This did not mean, however, that he was the most morally respectable. As the god of war, he acted transmoral or possibly amoral, inciting individuals, peoples, and deities against one another in many tales. For example, he was cited as the one to blame for the Battle of Bravellir and for the enmity between Harald Wartooth and his nephew, Sigurd Ring.

One-eyed and wearing a large-brimmed, low-hanging hat and blue cloak, Odin was said to be the god of magic, poetry, knowledge, and understanding in addition to being the deity of kings and of war. He rode an eight-legged horse, the offspring of Loki in mare form and the giant's stallion in the story from earlier in this chapter. Odin headed Valhalla, the famed hall that housed those who died in honorable battle.

His face was hidden from view in the tales that are told of him, and yet, Viking sagas tell tale of many interactions between humans and Odin. Not the least of these tales is one that recounts that Odin taught his protégés the *svinfylking*, or the "swine formation" for battle. This wedge-shaped formation was signature of warring Vikings in their offensive strikes.

Odin was married to Frigg, but he had many lovers. He seduced the giantess, Gunnlod, for example, and stole her mead of poetry to become to god of poetry, for example. Additionally, another tale tells of how he raped the earth goddess, Rinda, after she spurned his advances, and he was known to have a weakness for Freyja, one of the Wane goddesses.

Overall, Odin was a deity that broke the rigidity of what was considered normal by creatively and even destructively transgressing social boundaries.

Tyr – The Just God

Tyr was originally the god of war, though he was overshadowed by Odin in that respect. The rune representing his name, an upward arrow, was still used to confer victory in battle, however. He was also the deity of the Thing, which was the people's assembly locally, regionally, and nationally. He was considered the only moral god of the Viking pantheon, as the god of legal justice and oaths.

We can find a testament to his moral purity in Snorri Sturluson's recounting of the chaining of Fenrir the cosmic wolf. According to the tale that Sturluson recorded, Loki fathered a giant wolf named Fenrir that the gods took in to raise. Fenrir began to grow larger and more fearsome until the gods decided to chain him in unbreakable fetters. Fenrir grew angry and demanded to be freed. The gods promised that, should he not break free from the chains, they would free him themselves because that would show that he was harmless. Fenrir demanded a guarantee, and Tyr put forth his right hand in an oath of promise. Fenrir could not break free, but in the process of trying, he bit off Tyr's right hand. The gods did not free him, and it was said that all bit Tyr laughed at the results of the test.

We can see from this story that Tyr was the only god who attempted honesty and that his honesty was met with disdain and ridicule from the other deities. Thus, one can see how the Vikings concluded from their own stories that the gods were the ones to introduce moral failure and gullibility into the world.

Thor – The Strong God

Thor was another As deity that was very popular among the Vikings and in Norse mythology today. He was the god of thunder and lightning and storms. Unlike in our modern understanding of Norse mythology, Thor was not overtly called out as a son of Odin, nor as the brother of Loki.

In appearance, Thor was described as more youthful than the other gods, tall, red-bearded and handsome. The Vikings knew his personality to be of violent temper, tough as a warhorse, a strong beer drinker, and a ravenous eater. He was considered the strongest of the gods, at least physically speaking. He fought the giants of the sterile wastelands with his hammer, Mjollnir, and with his strength rather than by using trickery, as we know Loki and Odin were likely to do.

Thor possessed a team of goats upon which he rode up and down mountainsides and on the bridge from Asgard. When he was hungry, he would kill and eat the goats and then reanimate them with his hammer as long as none of the bones were broken.

Loki – The Trickster God

Loki's name comes from a word meaning "to close" as in "shutting or bringing to an end." He is the son of a giant, and by another giant, Angr-Boda (literally "grief messenger"), he sired three monstrous beings – Fenrir the wolf, the Midgard Serpent, and the goddess, Hel. The fate of these three offspring sealed the fate of the gods as Ragnarok in that Fenrir was chained, the Midgard Serpent was cast into the primordial sea, and Hel was banished to the Niflheim (literally "fog home" in the icy north) to become both the goddess and the realm of the dead. It was said that Loki would return with his sons and daughter to assault the As deities in Ragnarok.

In another story of Loki and his relationship with the other gods, Snorri Sturluson tells us of Loki's banishment and chaining to a cliff until the End Times. The story begins with Odin and Frigg's son, Baldr, having bad dreams about his own death, which caused Frigg to go to all the beings in creation and gather their oaths not to harm Baldr. Loki found out that the mistletoe plant was left out, and so he set up a competition in which he armed Hodr, Baldr's brother, with mistletoe, and he thus had Badlr killed, with Hodr paying for Baldr's death by forfeiting his own life.

At this point Frigg visits Hel and pleads with her to let Baldr return to the land of the living. Hel agreed she would do so if every living creature mourned Baldr's death. Every living creature indeed did mourn him, except for the giantess, Pokk, who was really Loki in disguise, causing Baldr's resurrection to be cancelled.

The gods then chased Pokk, or Loki, who then turned into a salmon but was eventually caught and chained to a cliff. A serpent spitting venom was set at the top of the cliff to torture Loki, whose writhing was said to cause earthquakes. In Ragnarok, Loki would break free and reign destruction on the deities and humanity along with his offspring.

Hans-Peter Hasenfratz again comments on the similarity between this Viking saga and the myths of Iran. A monster named Azdahag was said to have been chained to Damawand, the highest peak of the Alborz Mountains. His breaking free would initiate the battle between evil, of Ahriman, and good, Ahura Mazda, in the same way as Loki's breaking free would initiate the last battle called Ragnarok. In this way, we see that these two cultures likely influenced each other.

Frigg – The Women's Goddess

Frigg was Odin's wife and mother to Baldr and Hodr. Like many of the deities, being bound in matrimony to a husband, Odin, did not stop her from flirting with other gods and mythological beings like giants. She was said to have had relations with her in-laws, for example. She was the goddess of love and, in the more southern regions of the Viking traditions, was the women's goddess.

Frigg's role in the myth of the chaining of Loki is an important one, as it shows how the goddesses as well as the gods can overlook and fail morally. Her overlooking of the mistletoe plant killed Baldr and Hodr as much as Loki's sly ways, and so she was no exception to the fallibility of the Viking pantheon.

One myth that tells us a little of Frigg's personality and relationship with Odin is as follows: Odin received a gold statue, presumably from a lover, and in jealousy and in desire of adornment, Frigg demanded that the gold statue be torn down, melted, and turned into gold jewelry for her use. Odin conceded.

Chapter Five: Viking Deities – The Wanes

For the most part, the Wanes seem to have been fertility deities. Incest was a common theme among the Wanes, though the Ases looked down upon the practice. The Wanes therefore took wives and husbands in non-incestuous relationships but continued their sibling-romantic relationships as lovers outside of their marriages.

Some of the more commonly mentioned Wane deities include: Njordr and his sister, Freyr, Freyja, Idun, and possibly Nerthus.

Njordr and His Sister – The First Incest

Njordr was a fertility deity who had an incestuous relationship with his sister, who was not named in any tales associated with him. Through their sexual relationship, Njordr gave seed to the two main fertility gods, Wanes also who went by the names of Freyr and Freyja. Njordr was the god of abundance, and worship of him conferred safe journeys at sea with plentiful catches of fish. He was also thought to govern the wind.

Because the As deities looked down on sibling marriage, Njordr married the daughter of a giant, the daughter's name being Skadi. Skadi enjoyed the cold mountainous regions of the land and skiing down mountainsides, while Njordr enjoyed the sea, so the two lived apart in their unhappy marriage. Njordr's residence was supposed to have been called Noa-tun, or "ship town."

Freyr – The God of Fertility

Freyr was born to Njordr's sister by the seed of Njordr, along with his twin sister, Freyja. He was *the* fertility god, though other deities of fertility existed in the Scandinavian pantheon. His name means something like "the one who is first" or "the one who is lord."

Vikings considered him to be the deity that bestowed peace and pleasure upon humankind, and a variant of his name, "Frodi," was associated with a mythical, primordial king of peacefulness, idealized to be certain. Freyr's animals were animals of fertility, namely the horse and the goat. Human sacrifice to Freyr was not uncommon and Saxo Grammaticus even reported that Freyr was the one to introduce human sacrifice.

Freyr had an incestuous relationship with his sister, Freyja, just as their parents had had relations with their sibling to bear them. However, just as Njordr married another woman than his sister to appease the As deities, so Freyr married Gerd, the giantess to appease the Ases. Gerd was not won easily, however, and it was said that it was only under the threat of his malicious magic that she agreed to become his wife.

Frejya – The Lover of the Gods

Freyja was Freyr's counterpart, twin sister, and incestuous lover, daughter to Njordr and his sister. Her animals parallel Freyr's animals: horses and pigs as well as the addition of cats. She was known for promiscuity, having been a lover to each of the gods and to some giants as well. Her relationship with Odin made Frigg jealous, as Odin had a weakness for Freyja and Freyja enjoyed his special favor. Freyja also shared her powers of malicious magic with Odin.

Frigg and Freyja shared a lot in common, it would seem. Besides their desire for Odin, they both had a desire for adornment in precious metals like gold. Four dwarves fashioned a necklace in one story and agreed to give it to Freyja is she slept with each of them. She did so and, thus, obtained the necklace. Odin, jealous of the dwarves and their relationship with Freyja, tells Loki to sneak in to steal the necklace. Loki sneaks in as a fly to Freyja's room and then turns into a flea to bite her to cause her to turn so he could access the clasp of the necklace, which he promptly stole.

One question that some historians have asked is whether Frigg and Freyja are in fact the same goddess. The reason for their question lies in the fact that Frigg and Freyja are etymologically the same in the southern parts of Vikings realms, such as in Germany, and because in the lower regions, only one of the two is mentioned. This leads historians and social scientists to agree that it might be that the Scandinavians made two goddesses out of one or, alternatively, in Germany, the two coalesced into one. In either case, Frigg and Freyja fill similar roles in Scandinavian mythology but remain unique in other senses.

Idun – The "Renewing One"

Idun was a Wane goddess who possessed the golden apples that were the food of the gods. She was the symbol of life and fertility to the Vikings, like many of the Wanes were. The golden apples she possessed were said to keep the gods young until the End Times, that is, until the great war of Ragnarok.

One story concerning Loki's trickery and slyness includes Idun. In the story, Loki kidnapped Idun at the behest of a giant and stole her golden apples, giving them to the giants. Then, upon seeing that the gods were aging very quickly without the golden apples, Loki and the other gods kidnap Idun from the giants and retrieve the apples, killing the giants in the process. This allows them to regain and maintain their youthful physique and appearance.

Nerthus – "Mother Earth"

Nerthus, the "Mother Earth" figure of the Wane detities, was said to have a temple somewhere on an island at sea. The priests of Nerthus would take her statue and transport it by wagon in a procession throughout the land, and while the procession occurred, peace would reign. Her name comes from the word *nerphuz*, meaning "under" or "below." She was believed to be a sustaining force below the Vikinsgs' feet, or a motherly, earth figure.

Upon further investigation, social scientists have concluded that Nerthus was likely the same as Njordr, or else she might have been his "unnamed" twin sister. Njordr and Nerthus both come from the same root word, and both are associated with the sea and peacefulness. For this reason, historians believe Nerthus grew out of the stories of Njordr rather than being a completely independent deity.

Chapter Six: Magic and Magical Practices

The Scandinavians believed in more than just deities as supernatural beings. Apart from the gods and goddesses, there were many other legendary creatures that existed within the mythos of the Vikings. These creatures included humans with magical powers.

The Vikings considered women particularly to be talented at magic. There were many types of magic in the Scandinavian world. These magics were not all labeled "dark" or "black," but generally, if the intent was aimed at the destruction or physical ailing of another person, the Vikings would call the ritual "black magic" or "dark magic."

Incantatory Magic

This type of magic focused on the spoken word as a method for invoking magical outcomes. Most spoken incantations were formulated in the past tense rather than in the present or the future because the Vikings believed that the precedence of a charm having worked before would increase the likelihood it could work again. This type of magical charm required repetition and was considered less powerful than other options.

Rune Magic

Rune magic was similar to incantatory magic except that the permanence of the runes rendered the magic more powerful and made repetition unnecessary. Runes were also written in past tense to increase the effectiveness of the charm. Sometimes the runes were encrypted to keep the wrong person from reading them, such as using acrostics or jumbling letters of a word.

Death Magic

Death magic, or necromancy, sounds like it would be automatically considered "black magic" or "dark magic" to an untrained ear, but in fact, death magic used by an individual's family was not considered dark at all. Rather, when a person *other* than a family member used a val-galdr (a death charm or death song, also called a "waking song") to revive a dead person, the magic turned on the reviver and the dead soul would wake to announce the reviver's doom.

Conjuration of the dead was used to ascertain future events as well as to gain knowledge of past truth. When using a val-galdr, a family member of the deceased was attempting to contact the soul of the dead person in Hel and bring their spirit back into their body to revive them. It was thought that a person gained power when they died, not over Fate so much as to know Fate, and the Vikings likely wanted to tap into that power.

Divinatory Magic

Divination magic was performed by wandering seeresses. They wore blue cloaks like the god of magic, Odin, and each carried her own staff. The seeresses were called *volvas*, after *volr*, meaning "staff." The volvas would eat a special diet consisting of only animal hearts, since the heart was seen as the seat of magical power and, by ingesting another being's heart, the seeress was supposed to increase her magical abilities.

The ritual for divination was conducted on a raised platform on which the seeress would enter a trance to commune with the gods.

Cursing Magic

Cursing magic was considered black magic when done with a group intention to harm another human being, such as when a criminal was outcast with cursing magic from a village. Outcasts and criminal were commonly the recipients of cursing magic, as were one's enemies.

One common practice of cursing magic was the making of a *nidstong*, or "scorn pole." In this ritual, one slaughtered a horse, cut off the horse's head, and attached the head of the horse to a pole that was placed in the ground. Then, a person muttered incantations or carved runes in the pole to make the magic more effective, though it seems even without incantatory or rune magic it might have been considered to work.

The reason the horse's head was used was that horse sacrifice was the most preeminent and effective sacrifice to the Vikings. The horse's head was turned to face the direction of the cursed person's abode, such that the horse was "looking" at them. If the person who was cursed by the magic saw the horse's head or read the runes, they could reverse the magic, it was believed.

Destructive Magic

Destructive magic was aimed at the destruction of another human being, and thus it was considered to be black or dark magic. Destructive magic was supposed to have originated with the gods, with the As gods learning it from a Wane goddess that they then used the magic to kill.

Other Magics

Other types of magic existed as well and some practices are detailed in Christian legal documents outlawing specific rituals and performances of magic.

For example, one Christian bishop specifically outlawed "love magic." In this type of magical practice, a woman would mix some of the blood of her menstruation into the food she was cooking for her husband and serve it to him together with a meal. This was thought to increase his love for her because the blood was the substance of magic and life to the Scandinavians and to ingest another person's blood was to ingest their essence.

Another type of magic that was common was "weather magic." This type of magic was intended to control weather patterns and was used mostly by farmers or those interested in crop yields.

A dark magic practice that many believed was constantly at play was the sending of one's soul or of one's psychic forces into an animal or bug. Doing do, a person would creep into another's room and "ride" their soul in a destructive, nightmarish experience that left the victim exhausted and terrorized the next day.

This was the type of magic that Loki employed when sneaking in to steal Freyja's necklace at the urging of Odin. First, he projected his psychic energy into a fly to sneak into Freyja's room and, when he saw that she was sleeping with her neck on the clasp, he moved his energy to a flea, biting Freyja to make her turn over.

Vikings commonly thought that a person could project their soul into a spider, a bear, or other animals, and that they would do so as fit their needs. Someone needing strength in battle would project into a bear's body and fight with the strength and ferocity of the bear. Someone trying to sneak into a room might become a spider.

Finally, another form of magic that existed and that many Scandinavians feared was that of werewolves. In the North especially, this type of dark magic that turned men and women into werewolves was a source of great terror.

Chapter Seven: Other Supernatural Beings

In addition to human beings with magical powers, other legendary creatures populated the Scandinavian mythos. Some of these creatures included dwarves, elves, wights, giants, the Norns and the landscape features like mountains and wells.

Dwarves

There are a couple origin stories for dwarves, one being in the *Poetic Edda* and saying tha the dwarves were made from the blood and bones of the giant,Ymir. In Snorri Sturluson's *Prose Edda*, the dwarves were more like parasitic pests that infested the giant Ymir's body and grew when he was killed.

The dwarves had various roles in the few stories where we encounter them in the *Poetic Edda* and *Prose Edda*. The four dwarves, Nordri, Sudri, Austri, and Vestri, or "North," "South," "East," and "West" in Old Norse, were said to hold up the vaulted ceiling of the sky. In other stories, they created the mead of poetry that Odin stole and drank, and they forge Mjollnir, Thor's hammer as well.

Elves

Elves were first discovered by modern historians in the *Prose Edda* recorded by Snorri Sturluson. It seems that Icelandic sources are rich with references to Elves, though the rest of Viking culture in Scandinavia only rarely, if ever, mentions elves, or *alfar*. The reference in Snorri Sturluson's work that most historians cited as evidence for the Vikings' belief in elves, however, has been un-substantiated.

Instead, we look to the *Elder Edda* for information about elves. Elves were considered nearly-human in many ways, and might even have been the dead spirits of humans in some reckonings. Volundr was a character identified as an elf in the work, *Volundarkvida*. Elves were often associated alliteratively with the Ases, and it seemed Freyr was somewhat associated with the elven beings, having taken over *Alfheimr*, literally "elf-world."

Elves were considered super-human and supernatural in a few senses, mostly in the sense that they were more beautiful and wiser than their human counterparts.

Wights

Wights were technically any sentient, living creature, thus including the elves, the dwarves, the giants, the gods, and human beings. However, in Norse mythology, when a person referenced a *vettr*, or wight in Old Norse, they were referring to a specific supernatural being that was tied to a certain aspect of nature, such as the land wights.

Land wights, or *landvaettir*, guarded specific areas of land in Viking mythology. Because of this, Vikings would take the carved dragon heads off the front of their long-ships before coming into port in order to not frighten and provoke an attack by the land wights.

The four land wights of Iceland are still found on its coat-of-arms. A troll-bull, a troll-eagle, a dragon, and a handsome giant were considered to be the four wights that protected the island of Iceland from attack and other disasters.

Giants

Giants represented the infertile regions of the world: the rocky places and the northern icy areas, and generally any hostile region that the Vikings could imagine. Giants lived in the circle of the Nine Worlds called Jottunheim, or alternatively, they lived in Utgard, depending on the conception of the world under which the specific Viking was operating. In either case, they were banished by the Ases to another realm and locked out of Asgard in a rebellion by the gods against their giant forefathers.

The Ases and the giants had a very complicated relationship, as shown in the *Poetic Edda* and the *Prose Edda*. Thor, Odin, Loki, and many other Ases were birthed by giantess mothers, and often were sired by giant fathers as well. The As deities rebelled against their parents, killing one giant named Ymir, for example, to create the world. Freyr and Thor, in particular, opposed the giants and guarded their worlds against them.

The giants' origin is said to have been in the birth of Ymir from the meeting of the mists of Niflheimr, the land of ice, and the heat of Muspellsheimr during the time of the Ginnunga Gap. Other giants were formed from Ymir's armpits and feet. Odin and the other gods saw their birth from another giant, Buri, and proceeded to murder Ymir and form the world from his remains.

The giants had a special connection to nature such that we might even consider them nature gods, though the Vikings would object to the terminology. With Ymir's body an essential part of the creation of the world, Hraesvelgr the eagle-shaped giant who governed the wind, Jord the mother of Thor and of animal and plant life, and Aegir and Ran seen as the sea personified, it was clear that giants had a deep relationship with the natural world.

Despite the god-like qualities that the giants possessed, they were not worshipped but instead seen as the opposition to the good of mankind and of the gods. In the final battle of Ragnarok, for example, the fire giants would launch an attack on the world, setting it on fire as a means of final destruction.

The Norns

The norns were mysterious, female beings that controlled the fate of the world and of individuals. Snorri Sturluson's account of the three most important norns described them as unmarried, maiden giantesses of great power. Their arrival from Jottunheimr brought an end to the golden age of the As deities.

The most important norns were named Urd, meaning "has become," Verdandi, or "becoming," and Skuld, or "should occur." They were said to have stood at the Well of Fate, drawing water and pour sand and water over the branches of Yggdrasill to prevent its branches from rotting. The three Norns were considered to have the most power among the deities, higher than the pantheon of Ases and the group of Wanes. In fact, the gods could not control the three Norns, but instead their power came from knowing Fate rather than from influencing it.

There were more than just the three Norns, however, and Vikings supposed that norns showed up at the birth of each child to determine its past, present, and future. It is unclear whether the modern understanding of the norn beings is accurate to the Viking system of beliefs. According to some Scandinavian writings, "norn" could simply be another word for "woman" and was used interchangeably at times.

Worship of Nature

Natural landmarks were also objects of worship and seen as supernatural in many cases. It is clear that Vikings often worshipped in groves rather than in constructed temples. There are also signs of worship on mountains and at certain wells. The remains of these rituals are often runes that have been carved into a stone or into the landscape, such as on a mountain face.

Chapter Eight: Viking Beliefs – Ragnarok

There are various references in the *Prose Edda* and *Poetic Edda* to a final day of destruction called "Ragnarok," meaning the "fate of the gods" or the "twilight of the gods." There are also runestones and other pictures that depict the scene portrayed in the Eddic texts. Before we look at the evidences for the Ragnarok saga's importance in Viking culture, let us seek to understand what was meant by the event.

The Sequence of Events in Ragnarok

Also called "Gotterdammerung" in German and made more famous by the composer, Richard Wagner's opera by that name, the "Twilight of the Gods" would begin with the destruction of social ties according to the poem, *Voluspa*, in the *Poetic Edda*. A volva, that is, a seeress with divination magic, begins to tell Odin in stanza 41 of the poem about the start of Ragnarok.

She describes three roosters crowing to signal the beginning of the end, one crimson rooster in a forest in Midgard, a golden rooster in Vahalla, and a soot-red rooster in Hel. Next, Garmr, the blood-stained wolf guardian of Hel, breaks free and runs such that brothers fight brothers and social ties break down.

Next, Asgard starts to break down, with Heimdall blowing the horn, Gjallarhorn, to alert the Ases to danger. Fire giants come forth from Muspellheim. The Ases take council with each other as the land of Jotnar, that is, of the giants, becomes tumultuous. Cliffs open and swallow giantesses, and the giants begin to advance on Asgard.

The giants and the gods begin to fight after this, including the Wanes. Freyr is killed by Surtr, the fire giant whose sword shines brighter than the sun. Fenrir the cosmic wolf breaks loose along with his father, Loki, and his siblings, Hel and the Midgard Serpent. Odin spears Fenrir but it is not a lethal blow, so Fenrir swallows Odin whole. Thus, Frigg witnesses her second great sorrow, the death of Baldr being her first sorrow. Vidar, Odin's son, kills Fenrir in a rage and thus avenges his father's death.

Thor attacks the Midgard Serpent, who has been causing huge waves by heaving his body in the primordial sea. Thor ends up killing the Midgard Serpent but is mortally wounded in the process. He takes nine steps after he kills the Serpent and then falls down dead himself. Heimdall takes on Loki and they each mortally wound the other before dying themselves.

As the gods meet their deaths, so does the world meet its destruction: stars fall from the sky, the sun is extinguished, and the earth is swallowed by the primordial sea. Flames from the fire giants' abode reach the heavens and everything goes up in flames.

Post-Battle Ragnarok: The Rebirth

In the aftermath of the Battle of Ragnarok, the world is reborn. The volva reports to Odin that she sees the earth emerging from the water and the surviving Ases congregating on the field of Idavollr. They find that the fields regrow on their own and the Ases rediscover the golden game pieces with which they used to play in their golden age. Hodr and Baldr return and resurrect Thor and the other sons of Odin.

A mortal man and woman appear, having hidden in a forest. Their names are Lif and Lifprasir, and they repopulate the earth under the headship of a new deity that appears to be of Christian influence, a new and preeminent "All-Father." Apparently, the new deity is from "above" the courts of the gods, and is said to rule over everything, being powerful and mighty.

Written Sources of Evidence of Ragnarok Beliefs

As mentioned earlier, there are various sources in Scandinavian and Viking historical artifacts that aide our understanding of Ragnarok. The *Prose Edda* and the *Poetic Edda* are just two of these sources.

The Poetic Edda

Within the *Poetic Edda*, there are numerous poems that either reference or describe parts of Ragnarok. For example, the *Voluspa* records the volva's prophecy to Odin of the Fate of the Gods. Additionally, *Vafprudnismal* talks about the aftermath of the Battle of Ragnarok, telling of how the sun goddess, Sol, will bear a daughter who will continue on her mother's path after Fenrir consumes Sol. Odin gains much knowledge from Vafprudnir in this poem, as do we, concerning the resurrection of Odin's and Thor's sons and other finalities.

The Prose Edda

Within the *Prose Edda*, Snorri Sturluson quotes the *Poetic Edda* heavily but sometimes contradicts what the *Poetic Edda* tells us about Ragnarok and other beliefs of the Vikings. *Gylfaginning*, one of the sagas that Sturluson records, speaks greatly to the theme of Ragnarok. In Chapter 51 to 53 of the saga, the figure named High, the king of the hall, tells Gangleri, a disguised King Gylfi, that Fimbulwinter (three winters in a row without summer) will mark the beginning of the Fate of the Gods. The saga, *Gylfaginning,* also talks about what places will survive the Battle of Ragnarok, and it says that Vidarr and Vali, Odin's sons, along with Baldr and Hodr, will live on the field of Idavollr, which is in the place of the destroyed Asgard.

Other Sources of Information about Ragnarok

There are several physical artifacts and pictures that also depict scenes from Ragnarok that archaeologists have discovered as evidence and for further illumination of the Vikings' beliefs about the End Times. These include: Thorwald's Cross, the Gosforth Cross, the Ledberg stone, and the Skarpaker stone.

Thorwald's Cross

Thorwald's cross is a runestone that was found on the Isle of Man in the British Isles. Partially surviving, it depicts a bearded man shoving a spear at a wolf, who has his right foot in its mouth. The large bird on the man's right shoulder is interpreted to be a raven, making the man Odin and the wolf Fenrir. This artifact dates between 940 and the 1099 A.D.

On the opposite side is a depiction of Christ triumphing over Satan with a large cross. The figure of Christ is very similar to the picture of Odin on the front of the stone, making this a piece of "syncretic art" that combines pagan and Christian beliefs.

The Gosforth Cross

This artifact was found in Cumbria, England and dates to between 920 and 950 A.D. It is a standing cross and is carved on all sides, in typical Anglo-Saxon fashion. However, though there are Christian scenes such as a depiction of the crucifixion, there are other scenes on the cross that seem clearly Nordic showing scenes from Ragnarok.

The style of the art even seems to be Borrish, or in the style of the Vikings. On the north side is a scene that many scholars believe to be a depiction of Vidarr fighting Fenrir.

The Ledberg Stone

This stone is similar to Thorwald's Cross but was found in Sweden and dates to the 11th century. On it is a carving of a figure with his foot in the mouth of a beast with four legs, presumably Odin with his foot in Fenrir's mouth.

The more notable feature of this stone is the inscription, which is highly encoded runes that scholars consider to be a "magic formula" that follows the common memorial dedication runes.

The Skarpaker Stone

The Skarpaker stone was discovered in Sodermanland, Sweden. It is from the sometime between 1000 and 1100 A.D. On the stones are the memorial runes written by a father for his dead son. It read alliteratively in the *fornyrdislag* poetry form that was reminiscent of the *Poetic Edda*, and scholars believe that, at the time the inscription was engraved in the stone, anyone who read it would be reminded of Ragnarok and find the expression of grief appropriate.

Chapter Nine: Viking Religious Practices and Rituals

Scandinavian society practiced a variety of religious and non-religious rituals, though many of the practices were tinged with influence of spiritual beliefs. Whether directly religious or simply influenced by beliefs about the world and the gods, Viking rituals had a depth of meaning that many a modern person fails to recognize. Behind the helmeted plunderers of Europe stood families and a daily life to which the warriors hoped to return.

Their lives consisted of religious rituals and private practices that defined their mentality and shaped their belief system. Growing up in Viking society made young men and women into Vikings, and, as they grew, they taught the younger generation what they themselves has learned. This self-perpetuation should be familiar, as it happens in every culture. While the practices themselves might seem a bit alien to us, we should seek to understand how each ritual perpetuated the culture from which it was birthed. That is, we ought to try to connect the dots between practice and belief and vice versa, as this will lead to greater insight into the nature of Viking life.

Viking Religion

Viking religion was decentralized for the most part and is considered a "folk religion," meaning it did not have a rigid organization. There were no official priests. Instead of an official organization of priesthood, the leaders of the communities from kingdom down to family took charge of the practice of the religion and of officiating ceremonies and rituals.

This speaks to the fact that the Vikings did not seem to distinguish between "religion" and everyday life. There was no word for "religion" in Old Norse until the Christians arrived because, although the belief system among the Vikings was by no means uniform, it was assumed nonetheless to exist in *some* form.

Worshipping the Gods

Odin

Worshipping Odin took a few forms. For one, he was called "the Hanging God" because of the way his worshippers performed their worship of him. First, they would mark the person who was to be used as a mock sacrifice or as a real sacrifice with a spear. Then, they would perform a mock hanging but using a piece of rope and hanging the sacrifice from a tree.

On occasion, the mock hanging would turn into a real hanging, if things went awry. This was taken to be a sign that the gods required a sacrifice in order to be appeased.

Another way in which the Vikings worshipped Odin was by "carving the blood eagle," a rather bloody practice in which they would sacrifice a person by cutting open their back and spread their ribs apart to allow the lungs to become "wings" while the sacrificed individual bled to death.

Finally, the worshippers of Odin might have sacrificed a horse or an eagle in place of a human sacrifice in order to please the god. They would kill the animal without breaking any of its bones and ingest the meat of the animal in order to partake of Odin's essence.

Thor

To sacrifice to Thor, one would most likely choose a goat, as this was Thor's animal. Again, the sacrificial goat would be killed, as Odin's horse or eagle was, and the meat of the goat would be ingested.

One important feature of the sacrifice was that the bones would not be broken, such as to eat the marrow of the goat's bones. This was in order that the goat could be revived in the afterlife, and it is explained in the story of Thor and the goat whose leg was broken in death and who therefore came back with a limp.

Freyr

Freyr's animals were the boar and the horse, so often one or both of those two types of animals would be offered in worship of Freyr.

Being the god of fertility, he was also associated with a giant phallus at the great temple of Gamla Uppsala. According to Adam of Bremen, who reported about the great temple in Gamla Uppsala to Thor, Odin and "Fricco" (presumably Freyr), worship of Freyr included obscene acts. Saxo Grammticus reports that Freyr introduced human sacrifice to the Scandinavians, and it was to Freyr and to Odin that most human sacrifices were made.

A tale of Gunnar Helming tells us more about the worship of Freyr. According to the tale, Gunnar Helming was accused of murder in the 1200's A.D. and sought refuge in the temple of Freyr. In the process of seeking refuge, he smashed the idol that was in procession and impregnated the temple priestess who was acting as Freyr's wife. When it was found that the priestess was pregnant, people took it as a sign of a good year and the charges against Gunnar Helming were dropped. Helming and the priestess then sought refuge in Norway and became baptized as Christians.

What the story tells us is that there were cultic processions with the image of Freyr to promote fertility in various regions. In addition, priestesses acted like the wives of Freyr according to this story and might have done so for other gods.

One final story that might give some insight into Freyr's worship rituals comes from 13th or 14th century Iceland. In the story recounted by a Christian source, the witness said that they saw a peasant town passing a horse phallus with a leek wrapped in cloth from person to person. Each person who received the object would tell an obscene poem. It is unclear whether this is simply Christian propaganda against pagan rituals or whether it had some truth to it.

Places of Worship

It is unclear whether there existed dedicated spaces or places for religious worship and activities, as there existed no pre-Christian words for "temple." Instead, it seems that the Vikings erected multifunctional buildings which served both religious and political as well as social purposes. This is consistent with the fact that the Scandinavians did not distinguish between religious beliefs and beliefs that influenced and shaped their everyday lives.

Multifunctional Regional Complexes

Some of these multifunctional centers have been found at various locations throughout Scandinavia, such as the most famous center in Gamla Uppsala in Upland, Sweden. Other locations include Borg in Lofoten, Uppkara in Scania, Gudme in Funen, and Lejre in Zealand. These complexes were likely used for large gatherings throughout regions rather than just for local use, and they included a mead hall attached to a smaller building connected by a fenced-in area.

Local Centers of Worship

Locally, the people worshipped differently than in the large centers for feasting. There were a few places that Vikings worshipped locally. First, there were holy spaces, such as an area marked by stone or a branch fence. This area was then combined with certain rules, such as the outlawing of spilling blood on the holy ground. Vikings saw the local village as a microcosm of Asgard, Midgard, and Utgard, with Asgard and Midgard being in the village itself and Utgard being the frightening, dangerous outside world. People also worshipped in sacred groves and at wells and mountains, sometimes leaving offering at trees, streams, and rocks, possibly to the land wights.

Local Structures for Worship – Hofs, Horgrs, Sals, and Ves

Hofs, roofed halls, or *horgrs*, possibly made of a heap of stones, were likely a center for religious activity in the village but were not exclusively used as such and some religious activity happened outside these sites as well.

The *sal* (or hall) was another place that might have been used for worship, as was a multifunctional hall. Sals were longhouses with one room and was considered a prestigious center for religious ritual. Often it was connected with political power and with the god, Odin.

The *ve* was a different type of holy place and comes from the word *wiha,* literally meaning "holy." Thus, it is no question whether this type of site was used for religious purposes. Most originally this was probably used to describe holy places in nature but later the Vikings might have used the term *ve* to describe religious buildings that they had built as well.

Religious Leaders

There existed no class of priests and priestesses nor was there a stratum of society that functioned as exclusively religious leaders. Instead, there were various political and social roles that doubled as religious leadership among the Vikings.

The *godi* and *gydja* were the words for "priest" and "priestess" in Iceland and throughout the Scandinavian world. It also meant "chieftain," as the religious leader was aso connected with politics and the jurisdiction of the law. A godi, therefore, was a politician, a judge or jurist, and a spiritual and religious expert.

The kings and jarls were not only in power politically but were responsible for the spiritual and religious well-being of their people. They led the aspects of public faith while the head of the household led the family in the private aspects of religious practice.

There were a few other types of religious leaders in the Viking world. The *pulr*, or thul, was somehow related to reciting songs or speeches, so they might have functioned as the keepers of sacral knowledge, like bards. The pulr or thul also had connections to Odin, the god of kings and of poetry, and so the thuls might have been involved in banquet hall life.

The *volva* and the *seidmadr*, both connected with divination magic, were associated with a type of sorcery called the *seid*. Their magic and religious associations were connected to both Odin and Freyja, originating with Freyja according to myth.

Chapter Ten: Rituals of Life Events – Rites of Passage

Various rites of passage such as birth, marriage, and death, were, unsurprisingly, accompanied by religiously focused rituals. Strangely, no records indicate that there was a rite of passage from childhood to adulthood, or at least there was no ceremonial recognition of such events recorded by the Vikings that we have discovered.

Birth

Birth was a very dangerous experience for both the mother and the child. Aa a result, it was ordinary practice to perform birth rites surrounding a pregnancy and the birth of a child. When a woman gave birth among the Vikings, it was common that the people would pray to the goddesses, Frigg and Freyja and sing *galdr* songs, or "spell" songs in order to protect the mother and baby from the dangers of childbirth.

Vikings believed that at the moment of birth, a child's fate was determined by the Norns. This might have influenced the fairy tale that many know about Sleeping Beauty, in which the "fairy godmothers" determined the female child's blessings and curse in life.

Nine nights after a child was born, another ritual occurred. The child was placed on its father's knee. The participants in the ritual would then sprinkle the baby with water and the father would name the child. Names were highly symbolic and often included the names of ancestors and of deities.

Once this ritual was performed, the socially acceptable means of limiting the population by exposing a child to the elements was no longer an option. Instead, leaving the named and accepted child would be considered to have been murdered should the parents allow it to be "exposed."

Marriage

Marriage and weddings were quintessential to Viking life.

The engagement process was a ritual in itself. To begin the process, the groom's family would send some delegates to the bride's family to propose. The betrothal was then set and the dowry, or *heimanfylgja,* and the groom's wedding present to the bride, or *mundr*, were decided. There remained became and remained the bride's property. The dealings ended with a feast which sealed the terms of the betrothal.

The wedding itself was more important and extravagant than the betrothal. Called a *brudlaup*, the wedding was a public gathering of the bride and groom's families in which there was feasting for three or more days. During the wedding, the goddess, Var, the goddess associated with oaths, witnessed the bride and groom's vows. In addition, a representation of Thor's hammer, Mjollnir, was placed in the bride's lap as a phallus to encourage blessing in marriage. Also, Freyr and Freyja were called as witnesses to bless the bride and groom in their fertility and love with each other.

On the first night of the wedding, the bride and groom were led to the bridal couch as one of the central rituals of the wedding. Witnesses who were carrying torches led the couple to their bedchambers that night.

Death and Ancestor Veneration

Vikings believed that, in death, a person could still influence his or her descendants. This was important, even essential, to the perceived well-being of a family, such that if a family treated their dead well, they were believed to have been blessed, while families feared displeasing their ancestors for the bad fortune their dead could bring on them.

The dead were buried in mounds, the size and shape of which was based on the status of the individual who had died. The mounds were made close to the living descendants of the dead person as a way or protecting against bad luck and for fertility's sake. The dead were often buried with sacred or costly objects to take with them into the afterlife. Historians believe that the offerings for the dead were continual, as the tombs and burial mounds show signs of having been reopened on occasion.

The offerings that the families made for their dead included food and drink. The race of creatures called *alfir*, or elves, were sometimes associated with the dead, and so some scholars believe that the elves were actually seen as the spirits of dead Vikings.

Chapter Eleven: Viking Society

Viking society was highly stratified and the classes influenced each other in unique ways. Daily life was determined by various factors, such as gender and class.

The Classes - Origins

There existed three classes in the Viking class system as well as a slave or servant class that fell outside the stratified system. There exists an Eddic poem that explains the origin of the class system as follows:

Rigr, an emanation of Odin, visited a childless woman and her husband, and in an act of guest prostitution, impregnated the wife. She gave birth nine months later to Praell, or "thrall," who married the woman, Pir, and thereby sired the race of thralls, or servants. These were technically outside the class system, not a fourth class.

Rigr then visited and slept with another married woman for three nights and she gave birth nine months later to Karl, a "man of low class." Karl grew up and then married, and he sired the race of karlar, that is, of freemen.

Rigr visited a final married couple, sleeping with the wife for three nights, and she became pregnant. Nine months later, she gave birth to Jarl, a "man of noble standing" or "a chief" or "warrior."

Jarl grew up to win the hand of a daughter of a hersir, which was a regional military leader. The woman who becomes his wife gives birth to Konr-ungr, a "young sproutling," who then becomes *Konungr*, or king.

The Classes – Roles

The thralls were are the bottom of the class pyramid, having the lowest social standing. According to the law, a master could beat his or her thrall to death but needed to announce the killing on the same day as it happened. A thrall was doomed to a hard life – they would work hard and were denied basic privileges like a burial when they died. Instead their bodies were left to the elements. Other times they were given more privileges, like being buried with their masters or becoming *bryti*, a farm steward. Thralls were essential to the running of Viking society.

Bondis or the karlar, freemen who were farmers, merchants, and skilled craftsmen, were the backbone of Viking society and had more influence than one might expect given monarchal nature of Scandinavia. The reason for this was that the jarls and kings needed the bondis' approval and allegiance to their cause. This was not taken for granted but instead earned through the gift economy and through the provision of protection by the jarl or king.

A bondi's main purpose in life was to advance his family's fame and fortune. They had the right to bear arms and did so in order to protect their families against other families in blood feuds, their lands against encroachment by other Vikings, and their kingdoms against invaders. In their free time, bondis hunted for both food and pleasure as well as practiced swordsmanship, archery, swimming, wrestling, and other physical sports.

Above the bondis or karlar class was the jarl class. These were powerful landowners and military men, the Viking aristocracy. Jarls owned very large tracts of land and leased the lands to bondis beneath them. Viking jarls had miniature kingdoms of sorts in that they provided protection in order to receive taxes from the bondis and also the bondis' support in disputes. The jarls were important in religious rituals in that they officiated many religious events, like priests. They also raised a *ledugen*, or levy, or men to lead in battle in protecting the land and bondis beneath them.

The King was the highest level of stratified society, the member of the highest class in the Viking class system. He led the jarls and gained his wealth through pillaging and plundering during raids as well as through levying taxes. He financed the *hird*, a standing army of professional warriors, in order to keep the feuding jarls in check.

The king had an obligation to the jarls and to the bondis to protect them and to lead them well. As such, while the king had ultimate authority, his power was tempered by the attitudes and allegiances of the jarls and bondis. The councils and assemblies that the bondis held, called Things, were also a means of keeping the King under the influence of the populace.

The Thing – Its Influence on Viking Society

The Thing as an assembly held by bondis, or land-owning freemen, in order to administrate the Vikings' law. Despite the fact that women had a high ranking and great amount of freedom in Viking society, only men could vote in the Thing.

Each district had its own thing, as well as every region. The Althing was the national assembly that ensured democracy was carried out. The Thing was the cornerstone of Viking government and ensured that the king and the jarls were in check.

The Thing would meet regularly and in times of need. Legal issues could be brought before such an assembly, but for any decision to be made, the Vikings required that the vote be unanimous.

Women in Viking Society

Women were considered highly capable and their input and contributions were valued considerably in Viking society. Scandinavian culture encouraged women to be self-reliant and self-motivating.

Though women could not vote in the local, regional, or national Things, they possessed a role unfamiliar to much of the female population of the world. For example, husbands made a very conspicuous show of when they handed over their keys to their wives for safe-keeping while they were out raiding and adventuring.

In addition, they retained many other rights that were might have been coveted by many of the rest of the world's women. Women were protected in Iceland by a law that required the minimum age of a woman be 12 years for her to marry. Also, women had the right to own property apart from their husbands and fathers. They could sue for divorce as well, and sue for their dowry to be returned in the process.

Women could choose their husbands as well in love marriages rather than in arranged marriages. Though arranged marriages did occur, women were often able to accept or deny a man's proposal of marriage apart from the will of her parents.

In general, Viking women were empowered and independent. They spent much of their days caring for their families: making food, spinning wool, making clothing, and performing other such tasks. However, they had a great deal of freedom and choice in the process of their lives. This empowerment led to their capability of handling the rough, unforgiving lifestyle of the northern lands of Europe.

Chapter Twelve: Viking Influence on Popular Culture Today

The Vikings and Scandinavian culture have must more far-reaching influence on culture today than the *Avengers* movies and contributions to our English language, though these are certainly some obvious impacts. In fact, the Norse mythology of the Vikings and culture in Iceland, Norway, Denmark and Sweden during the Viking Age have led to the naming of Bluetooth technology, Tolkien's mythos and the resulting fantasy genre of literature, impact in music such as the music of Richard Wagner, the names of weekdays in the English language, and even some of Nazi ideology, among other things.

"Bluetooth" Technology

The Swedish technology company, Ericsson, developed a way to connect two devices that would otherwise find no compatibility without wiring, such as a telephone with an earpiece and microphone piece. This technology they named, "Bluetooth," after Harald "Bluetooth" Blatand.

Harald Blatand was best known for constructing Danevirke, a series of blockades to keep wandering German barbarians form assaulting the Danish people. His lesser known accomplishment was that of uniting the Danish and Norwegian peoples, opening avenues of communication that would otherwise have remained closed. This was the reason for which Ericsson named their Bluetooth technology after him. In fact, the Bluetooth symbol combines th two runes that make up Harald Blatand's initials.

Contributions to the English Language

The Old Norse dialects contributed to the languages surrounding them, especially to modern English. The most obvious way the Viking language influenced modern English is in the weekdays: Tuesday, Wednesday, Thursday, and Friday. Tuesday was named after the god of justice, Tyr, whose name in Anglo-Saxon was *Tiw*. Wednesday was named for Odin, named *Wodan* in Anglo-Saxon. Thursday was, obviously, named for Thor, and Friday was the day of Freyja, or *Friga*.

Viking vocabulary also comes through in the English language in terms concerning war and violence. For example, the word for club was *klubba* in Old Norse, and the word for slaughter was *slatra*. Old Norse influence is also seen in many other types of English vocabulary. Words like sada, troll, and Hell (*Hel*) come from Old Norse and many animal names have direct relationship to Old Norse.

Many words in English for miry, boggy things come from Old Norse as well because Danelaw bordered swamps.

Danelaw was crucial in the influence of Old Norse on the modern English language. Not only did the Scandinavian rule in what is now modern Britain cause changes in vocabulary but also influenced sentence structure such that some linguists believe that English ought to be reclassified from West Germanic to be a North Germanic language along with Danish, Norwegian, Icelandic, and Swedish.

Films - Disney Movies, Pixar and the *Avengers*

Fairy tales and the resulting Disney movies seem to have a lot of Norse mythology and Scandinavian cultural influence. For example, one of the newest and most popular Disney princess films, *Frozen*, is based on a fairy tale, "The Snow Queen," whose main villain, the Snow Queen, was likely based on the giantess, Skadi, or might have drawn inspiration from the goddess of the world of the dead, Hel.

The movie, *Snow White*, also contains evidence of Norse influence. The seven dwarves who mine in the ground for jewels are reminiscent of Scandinavian dwarves who were also miners.

The Pixar movie, *How to Train Your Dragon* and its sequels are a direct reference to Viking culture. Many times, the characters mention Odin, their main deity. Of course, this is not completely accurate to what we have learned about Viking religious beliefs, seeing a Thor was more prominent in Viking theology than Odin, but this movie, nonetheless, shows Viking references in modern culture.

The *Avengers* movies, including the film, *Thor*, are another reference to Viking beliefs and culture. Thor, wielding a heavy hammer that he alone can lift, interacts with his father, Odin, and his adopted brother, Loki, in the first *Thor* film, travelling to Asgard and other worlds. This portrayal of Norse mythology is not accurate to Viking beliefs either but it reflects the fact that the modern person has some familiarity with Scandinavian beliefs enough to recognize some of the main players in Norse mythology.

Nazi Ideology

Under Adolf Hitler and Alfred Rosenberg, the Nazis dreamed of a trifunctional state, with Hitler as the ruler, the Nazis in the place of the jarls, the Aryan race as bondis, and the rest of the world in the place of thralls. They called in the Ordenstaat, or order-based state. Hitler often referenced the Germans Viking origins in relation to their destiny to be a people of conquest.

The Fantasy Genre in Literature and Gaming

The genre of literature that we know as fantasy or high fantasy has not always existed. Rather, it grew out of interaction with various mythos, not the least of which was the Norse mythology of the Vikings.

J.R.R. Tolkien

In conceiving and writing his extremely famous works, *The Hobbit* and *The Lord of the Rings*, J.R.R. Tolkien found a great deal of inspiration in the *Poetic Edda* and the *Prose Edda*. He conceived of various characters and objects in relation to Viking mythology. For example, Tolkien considered Gandalf the Grey, a wandering wizard, an "Odinic wanderer" with such parallels as a blue cloak and wide-brimmed, low-hanging hat to underline the similarities.

The dwarves and the elves of Tolkien's world of Middle Earth were modeled after those in Norse mythology, and the One Ring and the re-forged sword, Anduril, find their parallels in the *Volsungasaga*, in which we read about a ring of power, *Andvarinaut*, and a broken sword, *Gram*.

Tolkien's conception of Middle Earth and the sagas he recounts in *The Silmarillion*, *The Lord of the Rings*, and *The Hobbit* marked the beginnings of the fantasy genre in literature. This, in turn, created an entire genre of video games and gaming as well.

Dungeons & Dragons

The popular table-top role-playing game by *Wizards of the Coast*, Dungeons & Dragons, was based in the Tolkien mythos, which in turn was highly influenced by Viking beliefs and religion.

Many Viking monsters appear in Dungeons & Dragons as assailants and as creatures that must be overcome. These include trolls, fire giants, frost giants, dragons, werewolves, and many others. Though the creators of Dungeons & Dragons have created their own worlds in which they have built their own pantheons, the Norse gods and goddesses exist in many editions of the game as an alternate pantheon, complete with statistics to run them.

Perhaps more exciting to the players, dwarves and elves exist in the game as playable races of characters. This means that the player can play as elf or as a dwarf, with different features for each.

RPG (Role-Playing Game) Videogames

Almost any videogame that is a fantasy RPG, meaning that the player plays from the perspective of an individual character, has been influenced by Norse mythology. In the *Elder Scrolls*, for example, one can choose to play as an elf or dwarf, which are races from the Viking cosmology. Additionally, in *Dragon Age*, one can see the influence on playable characters as well as can spot the dragons as a reference to Viking culture.

Conclusion

Vikings were much more than simple marauding adventurers whose lives were centered on raping, pillaging, and plundering. These were certainly aspects of Viking culture, but their courage in battle was tempered by their fear of the Gods, wights and giants, their concern for their families, and their cautiousness toward destructive magic. Viking society was more complex and, in terms of women's rights, more forward-looking than the rest of the Europe at the time.

Viking morality was based in a different system than the rest of Europe and the world, but they had a collective conscience nonetheless. In them we can see many differences from ourselves, but we can also find many parallels and similarities: love for family and kin, desire for structure in society, fear of the unknown, and hopes for a better future for our children.

From Ginnunga Gap to Ragnarok, from Lindisfarne to the Battle of Stamford Bridge, from Kiev to Vinland and beyond, the Vikings have helped to shape and influence our modern world.

Lightning Source UK Ltd.
Milton Keynes UK
UKHW021437041222
413344UK00008B/100